MW01004066

101 More Things To Do With A Slow Cooker

101 ^Things MORE To Do With A Slow Cooker

BY
STEPHANIE ASHCRAFT
AND JANET EYRING

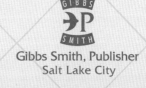

Gibbs Smith, Publisher
Salt Lake City

First Edition
15 14 13   20 19 18 17 16 15 14 13 12 11

Published by
Gibbs Smith, Publisher
P.O. Box 667
Layton, Utah 84041

Orders: (1-800) 748-5439
www.gibbs-smith.com

Designed by Kurt Wahlner
Printed and bound in Korea

Library of Congress Cataloging-in-Publication Data

Ashcraft, Stephanie.
  101 more things to do with a slow cooker / Stephanie Ashcraft and
Janet Eyring.—1st ed.
     p. cm.
  ISBN-13: 978-1-58685-293-1
  ISBN-10: 1-58685-293-0
  1. Electric cookery, Slow. I. Title: One hundred one more things to do
with a slow cooker. II. Title: One hundred and one more things to do with
a slow cooker. III. Eyring, Janet. IV. Title.
TX827.A82 2004
641.5'884—dc22

                    2004004527

Special thanks to all the
stay-at-home and working
moms who helped taste-test
these recipes.

Dedicated to our families, who
made this book possible.

CONTENTS

Chicken

Cajun Chicken Pasta 62 • Chicken Cordon Bleu 63 • Cheesy Chicken 64 •
Chicken and Dressing 65 • Citrus-Glazed Chicken 66 • Creamy Black Bean
Salsa Chicken 67 • Terisha's Chicken 68 • Greek Pita Chicken Sandwiches 69 •
Honey-Mustard Chicken Stir-Fry 70 • Chicken and Green Chilies 71 • All-day Salsa
Chicken 72 • Honey-Mustard Chicken Wings 73 • Chicken Stroganoff 74 •
Catalina Apricot Chicken 75 • Lemon-Honey Chicken 76 • Chicken
Alfredo Lasagna 77 • Wild Rice and Chicken 78

Beef

Beefy Cornbread Casserole 80 • Family Favorite Casserole 81 • Stuffed Pasta
Shells 82 • Grandma Brenda's Frito Pie 83 • Mouthwatering Meat Loaf 84 •
Grandma's Saucy Meat Loaf 85 • Barbecue Meat Loaf 86 • Hot Meatball
Subs 87 • Chili Dogs 88 • Mandarin Orange Steaks 89 • Gingerale Pot Roast 90 •
Italian Beef Roast 91 • Shredded Beef and Rootbeer Sandwiches 92 • Sweet-and-
Sour Meatballs 93 • Sweet-and-Tangy Twisted Beef 94 • Mexican Roast 95

Pork

Sweet Pork Ribs 98 • Orange-Glazed Pork Ribs 99 • Aloha Pork Chops 100 •
Cranberry-Sauced Cocktail Sausages 101 • Honey-Mustard Pork 102 • Pork
Chop Stroganoff 103• Polynesian Ham Steaks 104 • Cheesy Potato-and-
Ham Casserole 105 • Spicy Rice Casserole 106 • Supreme Pizza Lasagna 107 •
Southwestern Pork Wraps 108 • Asian Pork Wraps 109 •
Sausage Casserole 110 • Apple-Cranberry Pork Chops 111 •
Pork Roast with Apricot Dijon Mustard 112

Desserts

Country Peaches 114 • Golden Apple-Nut Cobbler 115 • Nutty Brownies 116 •
Cherry-Blackberry Cobbler 117 • Perfect Peach Cobbler 118 • Walnut-
Blackberry Delight 119 • Easy Blueberry Crisp 120 • Peachy Cherry Granola
Crisp 121 • Gooey Cherry Chocolate Cake 122 • Hot Fudge
Brownie Cake 123 • Dulce de Leche 124

HELPFUL HINTS

1. For healthier versions of slow cooker meals, use reduced-fat soups and reduced-fat or light sour cream and cream cheese. Ground turkey can be used in place of ground beef.

2. Ground beef or turkey should be browned and drained before adding to slow cooker.

3. Fresh milk, cream, sour cream, and cream cheese should be added during the last hour of cooking to prevent curdling. Evaporated milk does not curdle and can be substituted for fresh milk in most recipes.

4. Long-grain converted rice is recommended for rice dishes.

5. To test the cooking temperature of a slow cooker, fill it $3/4$ full of water, cover, and turn on high heat for 4 hours. With an instant heat thermometer, test water immediately after lid is removed—temperature should be at least 180 degrees. If it is lower, we recommend replacing the slow cooker. If it is higher, check all recipes for doneness after 3 hours of cooking time.

6. As a general rule, lifting the lid off the slow cooker lengthens the cooking time by 15 to 30 minutes.

7. Stirring is generally not necessary until time to serve.

8. Your slow cooker should be at least $1/2$ full to ensure proper cooking.

9. Recipes that contain raw poultry or beef should cook a minimum of 3 hours on high heat. Combinations of raw meat and fresh vegetables should cook at least 4 hours on high heat.

10. To make cleanup easier, spray the inside of the slow cooker stoneware with nonstick cooking spray before adding ingredients.

11. At cleanup, cool the stoneware liner somewhat before adding water; this will prevent cracking.

12. Adapting favorite oven recipes to a slow cooker:

Conventional Oven Baking Time	Slow Cooker High Cooking Time	Slow Cooker Low Cooking Time
15–30 mins.	1 1/2–2 hours	4–6 hours
35–40 mins.	3–4 hours	6–10 hours
50 mins.–3 hours	4–6 hours	8–18 hours

13. One hour on high heat is equal to 2–2 1/2 hours on low heat. (High heat=275–300 degrees; low heat=200 degrees. Heat varies from brand to brand.)

14. If your stoneware is removable, never place it on a hot stovetop burner.

15. Root vegetables (onions, carrots, potatoes, turnips) take longer to cook than meat. Place vegetables on bottom and around sides of slow cooker so they get the most direct heat.

16. Tough, inexpensive meat cuts work well. The moist, gentle heat slowly tenderizes these cuts as they cook.

17. Don't add more liquid than a recipe calls for, as liquid is retained.

18. If there's too much liquid at the end of cooking time and you want to thicken it, stir in some instant mashed potato flakes, instant tapioca, flour, or cornstarch.

19. Prepared jarred garlic may be substituted for minced garlic.

20. Recipes can be assembled and stored in the refrigerator the night before (unless they call for uncooked pasta). In the morning, place cold stoneware in cold electrical base. DO NOT PREHEAT ELECTRICAL BASE. Once stoneware is in place, turn to preferred heat setting.

21. To remove scratches from stoneware, use Bon Ami or vinegar and baking soda. Baking soda also works well to clean the electrical base. DO NOT SUBMERGE ELECTRICAL BASE IN WATER.

Happy slow cooking!

BEVERAGES

CHRISTMAS HOT CHOCOLATE

10 cups	**milk**
$3/4$ cup	**sugar**
$3/4$ cup	**cocoa**
$1/2$ teaspoon	**salt**
2 cups	**hot water**

Pour milk into $4^1/2$ to 6-quart slow cooker and turn on high heat. Mix together sugar, cocoa, salt, and hot water in a heavy saucepan. Boil 3 minutes, stirring often. Pour into milk and stir. Cover and cook on high heat 2–$2^1/2$ hours. Stir before serving. Makes 12 servings.

Serve with marshmallows and a candy cane.

STRAWBERRY-BANANA APPLE CIDER

I gallon	**apple cider***
2	**cinnamon sticks**
I package (3 ounces)	**strawberry banana gelatin**

Pour apple cider into 4^1/$_2$ to 6-quart slow cooker, then add cinnamon sticks. Cover and cook on high heat 3 hours. Stir in gelatin until dissolved. Keep on high heat I more hour. Turn on low heat to keep warm. Remove cinnamon sticks before serving. Makes 16 servings.

VARIATION: Substitute strawberry, raspberry, or peach gelatin in place of the strawberry banana.

* Apple juice can be substituted.

TROPICAL DELIGHT

1 bottle (64 ounces) **Hawaiian Punch**
1 can (8 ounces) **pineapple slices,** juice reserved
1 **whole nutmeg**
2 **cinnamon sticks**

Pour punch into 3^1/2 to 5-quart slow cooker. Add pineapple juice from can and set pineapple slices aside. Place nutmeg and cinnamon sticks in juice. Cover and cook on low heat 3–4 hours. Before serving, float pineapple slices on top of punch. Makes 9 servings.

AUTUMN BREW

I gallon	**apple juice**
I cup	**orange juice**
2	**cinnamon sticks**
5	**whole cloves**
4 to 5	**orange slices,** without seeds

Pour apple and orange juices into $4^{1}/_{2}$ to 6-quart slow cooker. Place cinnamon sticks, cloves, and orange slices in slow cooker. Cover and cook on high heat 3–4 hours. Turn on low heat to keep warm. Remove cinnamon sticks, orange slices, and cloves before serving. Makes 16 servings.

SPICY PEACH PUNCH

1 bottle (46 ounces)	**peach nectar**
2^1/$_2$ cups	**orange juice**
1	**cinnamon stick**
5	**whole cloves**
^{2}/$_3$ cup	**light brown sugar**
1 tablespoon	**lime juice**

Combine peach nectar and orange juice in 2^1/$_2$ to 4-quart slow cooker. Tie cinnamon stick and cloves in a cheesecloth bag and add to punch. Cover and cook on low heat 4 hours or high heat 2 hours. Stir in brown sugar and lime juice. Allow sugar to dissolve. Turn on low heat to keep punch warm. Remove cheesecloth before serving. Makes 9 servings.

DIPS AND FONDUES

SOUTHWEST BEAN PARTY DIP

$^1/_2$ to 1 pound	**ground beef,** browned and drained
2 cans (15 ounces each)	**refried beans**
2 cans (14.5 ounces each)	**diced tomatoes and chilies,** with liquid
1 package	**taco seasoning**
1 pound	**Velveeta cheese,** cubed

Combine all ingredients in greased $4^1/_2$ to 6-quart slow cooker. Cover and cook on low heat 3–4 hours or on high heat $1^1/_2$ hours, stirring every 30 minutes until cheese is melted. Makes 12–15 servings.

Serve with fresh flour tortilla strips or tortilla chips.

HOT MEXICAN PARTY DIP

1 to 2 pounds	**ground beef or turkey,** browned and drained
1	**large onion,** chopped
1 can (15 ounces)	**tomato sauce**
1 can (4 ounces)	**chopped green chilies,** with liquid
1 can (3 ounces)	**chopped jalapeño peppers,** with liquid
2 pounds	**Velveeta cheese,** cubed

Combine all ingredients in greased 4½ to 6-quart slow cooker. Cover and cook on low heat 3–4 hours or on high heat 1½-2 hours, stirring every 30 minutes until cheese is melted. Garnish individual servings with sliced olives, chives, and sour cream. Makes 12–15 servings.

Serve with tortilla chips.

ITALIAN SAUSAGE FONDUE

1/2 pound	**Italian sausage,** browned and drained*
2 jars or cans (14 ounces each)	**pizza sauce**
2 teaspoons	**Italian seasoning**
1 tablespoon	**cornstarch**
1 to 1 1/2 cups	**grated mozzarella cheese**

Combine all ingredients except mozzarella cheese in greased 2 1/2 to 4 1/2-quart slow cooker. Cover and cook on low heat 2–3 hours. Add mozzarella cheese before serving. Makes 8–10 servings.

Serve with bruschetta or breadsticks.

* Ground beef can be substituted.

CHILI-CHEESE DIP

$^1/_2$ to 1 pound   **ground beef,** browned and drained
1 can (15 ounces)   **chili,** with or without beans
1 pound   **Mexican Velveeta cheese,** cubed

Combine all ingredients in greased 3 to 4$^1/_2$-quart slow cooker. Cover and cook on low heat 3–4 hours or on high heat 1$^1/_2$–2 hours, stirring every 30 minutes until cheese is melted. Makes 6–8 servings.

Serve warm with tortilla chips.

RASPBERRY-CHOCOLATE-CARAMEL FONDUE

$1/2$ cup **seedless raspberry jam** or **preserves**
1 package (12 ounces) **semisweet chocolate chips**
1 jar (12 ounces) **caramel ice cream topping**

Combine all ingredients in greased 1 to 1$1/2$-quart slow cooker. Cover and cook on low heat 1$1/2$ hours, stirring every 30 minutes until melted and smooth. Cover and keep warm for serving up to 2 hours. Makes 6–8 servings.

Serve with bite-size cake pieces, bananas, apples, marshmallows, strawberries, grapes, or mandarin oranges.

If fondue is too thick, add evaporated milk by tablespoon until desired consistency is reached.

ROCKY ROAD FONDUE

1 1/2 tablespoons	**butter** or **margarine**
1 bar (10 ounces)	**chocolate with almonds,** broken
1 1/2 cups	**miniature marshmallows**
3 tablespoons	**milk**
1/2 cup	**heavy whipping cream**

Place butter, chocolate, marshmallows, and milk in greased 1 to 1 1/2-quart slow cooker. Cover and cook on low heat 1 1/2 hours, stirring every 30 minutes until melted and smooth. Gradually stir in whipping cream. Cover and keep warm for serving up to 2 hours. Makes 6–8 servings.

Serve with bite-size cake pieces, bananas, apples, marshmallows, strawberries, grapes, or mandarin oranges. Also great over ice cream.

SOUPS AND STEWS

SWEET BAKED BEAN SOUP

2 cans (16 ounces each)	**baked beans with molasses**
1 can (14.5 ounces)	**beef broth**
1 can (15 ounces)	**diced stewed tomatoes,** with liquid
1 tablespoon	**dried minced onion**
	salt and pepper, to taste

Combine all ingredients in lightly greased 2 to 3 1/2-quart slow cooker.
Cover and cook on low heat 4–6 hours. Makes 4–6 servings.

Serve with warm French bread.

FALL HARVEST CHOWDER

$1/2$ pound	**ground beef,** browned and drained
$1/2$ cup	**chopped onion***
4 cups	**water**
I cup	**diced carrots**
I cup	**diced celery**
I cup	**potatoes,** peeled and cubed
I can (28 ounces)	**diced tomatoes**
I can (8 ounces)	**tomato puree**
I teaspoon	**salt**
$1/4$ teaspoon	**black pepper**
$1/4$ teaspoon	**crushed bay leaves**
$1^1/2$ teaspoons	**Italian seasoning**

Combine all ingredients in greased $4^1/2$ to 6-quart slow cooker. Cover and cook on low heat 6–8 hours or on high heat 3–4 hours. For a thicker soup cook on low heat 8–10 hours. Makes 8–10 servings.

Serve in a bread bowl and garnish with freshly grated Parmesan cheese.

* $1/4$ cup dried minced onion can be substituted.

SOUTHWESTERN CHILI

¹/₂ pound	**ground beef,** browned and drained
1	**green bell pepper,** diced
¹/₂ cup	**chopped onion***
3 cups	**water**
1 can (16 ounces)	**pinto beans,** with liquid
1 can (16 ounces)	**black** or **kidney beans,** with liquid
1 can (10 ounces)	**tomatoes and green chilies,** with liquid
1¹/₂ teaspoons	**chili powder**
¹/₂ teaspoon	**cumin**
1 teaspoon	**salt**
¹/₄ teaspoon	**pepper**

Combine all ingredients in greased 4¹/₂ to 6¹/₂-quart slow cooker.
Cover and cook on low heat 6–8 hours or on high heat 3–4 hours.
Makes 6–8 servings.

Serve with Monterey Jack cheese and warm flour tortillas for dipping.

* ¹/₄ cup dried minced onion can be substituted.

FAMILY FRIENDLY CHILI

1 pound	**ground beef,** browned and drained
$^1/_2$	**large onion,** chopped*
1 can (14.5 ounces)	**diced tomatoes and green chilies,** with liquid
1 can (8 ounces)	**tomato sauce**
$^1/_2$ cup	**water**
1 tablespoon	**chili powder**
1 teaspoon	**salt**
$^1/_2$ teaspoon	**pepper**
$^1/_2$ teaspoon	**minced garlic**

Combine all ingredients in greased $2^1/_2$ to $4^1/_2$-quart slow cooker. Cover and cook on low heat 4–6 hours or on high heat 2–3 hours. Makes 4–6 servings.

Serve over corn chips with shredded cheddar cheese sprinkled over top.

VARIATION: Add 1 can (16 ounces) pinto beans.

* $^1/_4$ cup dried minced onion can be substituted.

VEGETABLE BEEF STEW

1 to 1¹/₂ pounds	**stew meat,** cubed
1 bag (8 ounces)	**baby carrots,** cut in thirds
2 cups	**diced potatoes***
1 can (15.25 ounces)	**whole kernel corn,** drained
1 can (14.5 ounces)	**green beans,** drained
2 jars (12 ounces each)	**beef gravy**
1 can (11.5 ounces)	**V8 juice**

Combine all ingredients in greased 4¹/₂ to 6-quart slow cooker. Cover and cook on low heat 6–8 hours or on high heat 4 hours. Makes 8–10 servings.

Serve with cheddar garlic biscuits.

* 2 medium potatoes equals approximately 2 cups of diced potatoes.

HUNGRY MAN STEW

1 pound	**ground beef, turkey,** or **sausage**
1	**medium onion,** sliced
2 cups	**diced carrots** or **baby carrots**
3	**red** or **russet potatoes,** diced
1 can (16 ounces)	**dark kidney beans,** drained
$^1/_4$ cup	**uncooked white long-grain converted rice,** not instant
1 can (8 ounces)	**tomato sauce**
4 cups	**water**
$^1/_4$ teaspoon	**chili powder**
$^1/_4$ teaspoon	**Worcestershire sauce**

Brown meat with onion, drain and pour in greased 3$^1/_2$ to 5-quart slow cooker. Combine remaining ingredients in slow cooker. Cover and cook on low heat 6–8 hours or until potatoes and rice are tender. Makes 8–10 servings.

Serve with warm cornbread and honey butter.

BACON-POTATO SOUP

6 cups	**potatoes,** peeled and diced
5 cups	**water**
2 cups	**chopped onions**
4	**chicken bouillon cubes***
6 slices	**bacon,** cooked and crumbled
I can (12 ounces)	**evaporated milk**
2 cups	**grated cheddar cheese**

Combine potatoes, water, onions, and bouillon cubes in greased 5 to 7-quart slow cooker. Cover and cook on low heat 6–8 hours or until potatoes are tender. Stir in crumbled bacon, milk, and grated cheese. Cover and cook an additional 20 minutes or until cheese is melted. Makes 10–12 servings.

Serve with hot biscuits and garnish soup with fresh chopped parsley.

VARIATION: Add $^{1}/_{2}$ cup diced celery and $^{1}/_{2}$ cup chopped carrots with potatoes at the beginning of cook time.

* 4 teaspoons instant chicken bouillon granules can be substituted.

SPICY POTATO SOUP

I pound	**ground beef or sausage,** browned and drained
4	**potatoes,** peeled and cubed
I	**small onion,** chopped
5 to 6 cups	**water**
3 cans (8 ounces each)	**tomato sauce**
$^1/_2$ teaspoon	**salt**
I teaspoon	**black pepper**
I teaspoon	**hot pepper sauce**

Combine all ingredients in greased 4$^1/_2$ to 6-quart slow cooker. Cover and cook on low heat 7–9 hours or on high heat 3–4 hours. Makes 10–12 servings.

Serve with a spinach and crumbled bacon salad with freshly grated Parmesan cheese.

VARIATION: Omit black pepper and hot pepper sauce and replace with I teaspoon Italian seasoning for a milder soup.

CHILI CON POLLO

3	**large boneless, skinless chicken breasts**
I jar (16 ounces)	**chunky salsa**
I can (15.8 ounces)	**Great Northern beans,** with liquid
I can (15 ounces)	**black beans,** with liquid
I can (14.5 ounces)	**diced tomatoes,** with liquid
2 teaspoons	**cumin**

Place chicken in greased 3^1/$_2$ to 5-quart slow cooker. Pour salsa, beans, tomatoes, and cumin over top. Cover and cook on low heat 6–9 hours. Break chicken into bite-size pieces with two forks before serving. Makes 8–10 servings.

Serve in bread bowls with a dollop of sour cream or guacamole.

VARIATION: Use hot salsa and diced tomatoes with green chilies for a spicy version.

CHICKEN TORTILLA SOUP

I pound	**boneless chicken,** cooked and shredded
I can (15 ounces)	**crushed tomatoes**
I can (10 ounces)	**enchilada sauce**
I	**medium onion,** chopped*
I can (4 ounces)	**chopped green chilies**
2	**cloves garlic,** minced
2 cups	**water**
I can (14.5 ounces)	**chicken broth**
I can (15 ounces)	**whole kernel corn**
I teaspoon	**cumin**
I teaspoon	**chili powder**
$1/4$ teaspoon	**crushed bay leaves**
I tablespoon	**dried chopped cilantro**

Combine all ingredients in greased $4^1/2$ to 6-quart slow cooker. Cover and cook on low heat 6–8 hours or on high heat 3–4 hours. Makes 8–10 servings.

Serve with tortilla strips and garnish with grated pepper jack cheese and guacamole.

VARIATION: Add I cup shredded carrots or shredded zucchini at the beginning of cook time.

* $1/2$ cup dried minced onion can be substituted.

CHEESY VEGETABLE SOUP

I can (10.75 ounces)	**cream of mushroom** or **cream of celery soup,** condensed
I can (12 ounces)	**evaporated milk**
$3/4$ cup	**water**
I tablespoon	**dried minced onion**
I cup	**Cheez Whiz**
4 cups	**frozen mixed vegetables,** thawed*

Combine all ingredients in greased $3^1/2$ to 5-quart slow cooker. Cover and cook on low heat 3–4 hours. Stir well before serving. Makes 6–8 servings.

Serve with sliced French bread.

* California blend vegetables can be substituted.

PORK CHILI VERDE

I pound	**pork stew meat***
I bottle (12 ounces)	**green taco sauce** or **salsa verde**
I can (14 ounces)	**black beans,** drained
I can (14 ounces)	**Great Northern beans,** drained
I can (4 ounces)	**chopped green chilies,** drained

Combine all ingredients in greased 3 to 4$\frac{1}{2}$-quart slow cooker. Cover and cook on low heat 6–8 hours or on high heat 3–4 hours. Makes 4–6 servings.

Serve with cheesy quesadillas.

VARIATION: Add $\frac{1}{2}$ cup chopped onion for more flavor.

* Beef or chicken stew meat can be substituted.

EASY BEAN SOUP

I can (15.5 ounces)	**Cannellini white kidney beans,** drained
I can (16 ounces)	**pinto** or **red beans,** drained
I can (15 ounces)	**black beans,** drained
2 cans (10 ounces each)	**diced tomatoes with green chilies,** with liquid
1/2	**onion,** chopped*
I can (14 ounces)	**chicken broth**

Combine all ingredients in greased 3 1/2 to 5-quart slow cooker. Cover and cook on low heat 6–8 hours or on high heat for 3–4 hours. Makes 6–8 servings.

Serve with crusty bread and herbed cream cheese spread.

VARIATION: Use diced Italian tomatoes in place of diced tomatoes with green chilies for a milder soup.

* 1/4 cup dried minced onion can be substituted.

Vegetarian Delights

ZESTY BEAN BURRITOS

2 cans (15 ounces each) **pinto beans,** with liquid
1 **medium onion,** chopped*
1 teaspoon **chili powder**
1 teaspoon **ground cumin**
$^1/_4$ teaspoon **cayenne pepper**
6 to 8 **flour tortillas**

Combine all ingredients except tortillas in greased 2 to 3$^1/_2$-quart slow cooker. Cover and cook on low heat 5–7 hours. Mash beans with potato masher. Spoon bean mixture onto center of warm flour tortillas. Makes 6–8 servings.

Serve with grated cheddar cheese, sour cream, and fresh salsa.

* $^1/_2$ cup dried minced onion can be substituted.

BROCCOLI-CHEESE CASSEROLE

1 package (10 ounces)	**frozen chopped broccoli,** thawed
3 cups	**cooked long-grain white rice**
1/4 cup	**chopped celery,** optional
1 can (10.5 ounces)	**cream of mushroom soup,** condensed
1 cup	**Cheez Whiz**
1/2 teaspoon	**salt**
1/8 teaspoon	**black pepper**
1/8 teaspoon	**garlic powder**

Combine all ingredients in greased 2 to 3 1/2-quart slow cooker. Cook on low heat 1 1/2–2 hours or until heated through. Makes 4–6 servings.

Serve with a tropical fruit salad.

CHEESY CAULIFLOWER FLORETS

1 bag (16 ounces) **frozen cauliflower florets***
1 can (10.75 ounces) **cheddar cheese soup,** condensed

Place frozen cauliflower in 3 1/2 to 4-quart slow cooker. Pour soup over top. Cover and cook on low heat for 4–5 hours. Makes 5 servings.

Serve with honey wheat rolls and jam.

* Frozen broccoli or a blend of broccoli, cauliflower, and carrots can be substituted.

CORN ON THE COB

6 to 8 **ears of corn,** in husks
$^3/_4$ cup **water**

Remove silk from corn but leave husks on. (If husks fall off, tie back on with kitchen twine.) Lay corn on its side in $4^1/_2$ to 6-quart slow cooker. Add water. Cover and cook on high heat 2–3 hours. Makes 6–8 servings.

Serve as a side to your meal of choice.

CHEESY POTATO CASSEROLE

7	**medium potatoes,** peeled and quartered
1/4 cup	**butter** or **margarine,** melted
1	**small onion,** chopped
1 teaspoon	**salt**
1 cup	**sour cream**
1 can (10.5 ounces)	**cream of mushroom soup,** condensed
2 cups	**grated cheddar cheese**

Topping:
1 package (6 ounces)	**herb-seasoned stuffing mix**
1/4 cup	**butter** or **margarine,** melted

Place potatoes in greased 4 1/2 to 6-quart slow cooker. Add butter, onion, salt, sour cream, soup, and cheese. Mix well. Pour stuffing mix evenly over potatoes and drizzle with butter. Cover and cook on low heat 6–8 hours or on high heat 3–4 hours. Makes 8–10 servings.

Serve with a crispy cucumber and vinegar salad.

AUTUMN CARROTS

2 pounds	**baby carrots**
$1/3$ cup	**brown sugar**
$1/3$ cup	**orange juice**
2 tablespoons	**butter** or **margarine,** melted
$2/3$ teaspoon	**cinnamon**
$1/8$ teaspoon	**nutmeg**

Place carrots in greased 2 to $3^1/2$-quart slow cooker. Combine other ingredients and pour over carrots. Cover and cook on low heat 3–4 hours or until carrots are tender. Makes 8–10 servings.

Serve as a side to your meal of choice.

For a thicker sauce: When carrots are done remove carrots from slow cooker with a slotted spoon and keep warm. Pour drippings from slow cooker into a small saucepan and bring to a boil. Add a mixture of $1/3$ cup water and 2 tablespoons cornstarch to saucepan. Return to a boil and pour over carrots before serving.

THANKSGIVING DRESSING

1 cup	**butter** or **margarine,** melted
1 1/2 cups	**chopped onion**
1 1/2 cups	**chopped celery**
2 packages (6 ounces each)	**seasoned stuffing mix**
1 can (14.5 ounces)	**vegetable** or **chicken broth**
2	**eggs,** beaten

In a large bowl, mix all ingredients together. Spread mixture into greased 3 1/2 to 5-quart slow cooker. Cover and cook on low heat 4–5 hours. Makes 10–12 servings.

Serve with your favorite Thanksgiving dishes.

This recipe can be easily doubled and placed in greased 6 to 7-quart slow cooker.

VEGGIE LASAGNA

12	**lasagna noodles,** uncooked
$^1/_4$ cup	**water**
I can (2.25 ounces)	**sliced olives,** drained
I can (4 ounces)	**mushroom pieces,** drained
$^1/_2$ cup	**shredded carrots,** optional
$^1/_2$ cup	**shredded zucchini,** optional
2 jars (26–28 ounces each)	**chunky vegetable spaghetti sauce**
I carton (16 ounces)	**ricotta** or **cottage cheese**
2 cups	**grated mozzarella cheese**

Break 4 noodles to fit in bottom of greased 6 to 7-quart slow cooker. Sprinkle half of sliced olives, mushrooms, and half of carrots and zucchini, if desired, over noodles. Then layer a third of the spaghetti sauce, half of the water, half of the ricotta or cottage cheese, and a third of the mozzarella cheese over top. Add another layer of noodles, second half of olives and mushrooms. Spread second third of spaghetti sauce and remaining water and ricotta or cottage cheese on top. Sprinkle another third of mozzarella. Layer remaining noodles, sauce, and mozzarella. Cover and cook on low heat 4–5 hours. Do not cook more than 5 hours. Makes 10–12 servings.

Serve with toasted French bread topped with melted Asiago cheese.

VEGETABLE SPAGHETTI SAUCE

1	**large onion,** chopped
8–10	**baby carrots,** cut in thirds
2 cans (4 ounces)	**mushroom pieces,** drained*
1	**green bell pepper,** seeded and chopped
2 cans (14.5 ounces each)	**diced Italian tomatoes,** with liquid
1 can (15 ounces)	**tomato sauce**
1 can (6 ounces)	**Italian-style tomato paste**
2 teaspoons	**sugar**
1/2 teaspoon	**salt**
1/2 teaspoon	**Italian seasoning**

Combine all ingredients in greased 3 1/2 to 5-quart slow cooker. Cover and cook on low heat 6–8 hours. Stir well. Makes 8–10 servings.

Serve over hot cooked spaghetti or bow tie noodles. Garnish with freshly grated Parmesan cheese.

For a thicker sauce, drain one of the cans of Italian tomatoes before adding to slow cooker.

* One 8-ounce package of fresh sliced mushrooms can be substituted.

THREE-BEAN CHOWDER

I can (16 ounces)	**kidney beans**
I can (16 ounces)	**fat-free refried beans**
I can (15 ounces)	**black beans**
I can (14 ounces)	**vegetable broth**
I can (14.5 ounces)	**diced stewed tomatoes,** with liquid
I	**medium onion,** chopped*
3/4 cup	**chunky salsa**
I teaspoon	**minced garlic**
2 teaspoons	**chili powder**
1/4 teaspoon	**cumin**

Combine all ingredients in greased 4 to 5-quart slow cooker. Cover and cook on low heat 6–8 hours. Makes 8–10 servings.

Serve with pita pockets stuffed with lettuce, rings of red onion, and green pepper slices.

* 1/2 cup dried minced onion can be substituted.

HONEY WHEAT BREAD

$^2/_3$ cup	**powdered milk**
2 cups	**warm water**
2 tablespoons	**canola** or **vegetable oil**
$^1/_4$ cup	**honey**
$^3/_4$ teaspoon	**salt**
I envelope (0.25 ounce) or $2^1/_4$ teaspoons	**active dry yeast**
3 cups	**whole wheat flour**
I cup	**flour**

In a bowl, dissolve powdered milk in warm water, then combine with oil, honey, salt, yeast, and half of both flours. With an electric mixer, beat on low speed 2 minutes. Add remaining flour and beat on low until combined. Place dough in greased 4 to 5-quart slow cooker. Cover and cook on high heat 2–3 hours. Makes 10–15 servings.

Remove stoneware from slow cooker and let stand 5 minutes. Invert bread onto a serving platter while still hot.

Serve with honey butter or your favorite jam.

CLASSIC WHITE BREAD

I envelope (0.25 ounce)
or 2^1/$_4$ teaspoons **active dry yeast**
I teaspoon **sugar**
^{1}/$_4$ cup **warm water**
I **egg**
^{1}/$_4$ cup **vegetable oil**
I cup **lukewarm water**
I teaspoon **salt**
^{1}/$_4$ cup **sugar**
3^1/$_2$ to 4 cups **flour**

In a bowl, combine yeast, I teaspoon sugar, and ^{1}/$_4$ cup warm water. Allow yeast to foam, about 5 minutes. Add egg, oil, lukewarm water, salt, ^{1}/$_4$ cup sugar, and 2 cups of flour. Beat with an electric mixer 2 minutes on low. With a wooden spoon, stir in the remaining flour. Place dough in greased 4 to 5-quart slow cooker. Cover and cook on high heat 2–3 hours. Remove stoneware from slow cooker and let stand 5 minutes before slicing. Makes 10–15 servings.

Serve with butter and your favorite jam.

CRANBERRY-ORANGE BREAD

$^2/_3$ cup **powdered milk**
2 cups **warm water**
3 cups **flour**
1 $^1/_3$ cups **sugar**
1 tablespoon **baking powder**
$^1/_4$ teaspoon **salt**
$^1/_4$ teaspoon **baking soda**
1 **egg,** beaten
$^1/_4$ cup **vegetable oil**
2 teaspoons **finely grated orange peel**
$^3/_4$ cup **dried cranberries,** coarsely chopped

In a bowl, dissolve powdered milk in warm water, then combine with 2 cups flour, sugar, baking powder, salt, baking soda, egg, and oil. Beat with an electric mixer 2 minutes on low. Add remaining flour and beat on low until combined. With a wooden spoon, fold in orange peel and dried cranberries. Place dough in greased 4 to 5-quart slow cooker. Cover and cook on high heat 2–3 hours. Makes 10–15 servings.

Serve warm with butter or a cream cheese spread.

TURKEY

HOLIDAY TURKEY

3 to 4 pounds	**boneless turkey breast**
I envelope	**onion and herb soup mix**
I can (16 ounces)	**whole cranberry sauce***
1/4 cup	**water**

Place turkey inside greased 3 1/2 to 5-quart slow cooker. Combine other ingredients and spread over top. Cover and cook on low heat 8–10 hours or on high heat 3–4 hours. Internal temperature will be 190 degrees when done. Makes 8–10 servings.

Serve with garlic mashed potatoes, steamed vegetables with lemon zest, and whole wheat rolls.

A turkey breast with bone can be used by increasing the cooking time to 10–12 hours on low heat. Check the internal temperature for doneness.

* Jellied cranberry sauce will not work in this recipe.

APPLE CIDER TURKEY

3 to 4 pounds **boneless turkey breast**
salt and black pepper, to taste
$^1/_3$ cup **apple cider***

Place turkey inside greased $3^1/_2$ to 5-quart slow cooker. Salt and pepper meat to taste. Pour apple cider over top. Cover and cook on low heat 8–10 hours. Internal temperature will be 190 degrees when done. Makes 8–10 servings.

Serve with cranberry sauce, favorite stuffing, salad, and rolls.

A turkey breast with bone can be used by increasing the cooking time to 10–12 hours on low heat. Check the internal temperature for doneness.

* Apple juice can be substituted.

CREAMY MUSHROOM TURKEY

3 to 4 pounds	**boneless turkey breast**
2 cans (10.5 ounces each)	**cream of mushroom soup,** condensed
1 can (4 ounces)	**mushroom pieces,** drained*
1 envelope	**dry onion soup mix**
1 cup	**sour cream**

Place turkey breast in greased 4½ to 6-quart slow cooker. In a bowl, mix remaining ingredients, except sour cream, and spoon over turkey. Cover and cook on low heat 8–10 hours. Internal temperature of turkey will be 190 degrees when done. An hour before serving, break turkey breast into large chunks with two forks. Stir in sour cream. Cover and cook for remaining hour. Makes 10–12 servings.

Serve over steamed brown rice with a side salad of iceberg lettuce, cauliflower, and radishes.

* ½ cup fresh sliced mushrooms can be substituted.

FRESH ONION TURKEY BREAST

3 to 4 pounds **boneless turkey breast**
I envelope **dry onion soup mix**
$^1/_2$ **medium onion,** thinly sliced

Place turkey inside greased 3$^1/_2$ to 5-quart slow cooker. Sprinkle soup mix over turkey. Layer onion slices over top. Cover and cook on low heat 8–10 hours. Internal temperature will be 190 degrees when done. Makes 8–10 servings.

Serve with hot green beans and a fresh spinach salad garnished with dried cranberries.

A turkey breast with bone can be used by increasing the cooking time to 10–12 hours on low heat. Check the internal temperature for doneness.

TURKEY OLÉ

4 cups	**shredded cooked turkey***
1 envelope (1 ounce)	**enchilada sauce mix**
2 cans (6 ounces each)	**tomato paste**
1/2 cup	**water**
1 cup	**grated Monterey Jack cheese**

Stir shredded turkey, enchilada sauce mix, tomato paste, and water together in greased 3 to 4 1/2-quart slow cooker. Cover and cook on low heat 3–4 hours or on high heat 1 1/2 –2 hours. Before serving, sprinkle cheese over meat. Makes 4–6 servings.

Serve with corn chips and garnish with sour cream, sliced green onions, and sliced olives. Recipe can also be used as filling for tacos or tostadas.

* Chicken can be substituted.

Chicken

CAJUN CHICKEN PASTA

I pound	**chicken tenders**
I can (15 ounces)	**crushed tomatoes,** with liquid
I can (6 ounces)	**tomato paste**
1/2 cup	**chopped red bell pepper**
1/2 cup	**chopped onion***
3 teaspoons	**minced garlic**
1 1/2 teaspoons	**Cajun seasoning**
1/4 teaspoon	**crushed bay leaves**

Combine all ingredients in greased 3 1/2 to 5-quart slow cooker. Cover and cook on low heat 6–8 hours. Makes 6–8 servings.

Serve over hot cooked pasta of your choice.

* 1/4 cup dried minced onion can be substituted.

CHICKEN CORDON BLEU

4 to 6 slices	**ham**
4 to 6 slices	**mozzarella cheese**
4 to 6	**boneless, skinless chicken breasts,** flattened to $^1/_4$-inch thickness
I can (10.75 ounces)	**cream of chicken soup,** condensed
$^1/_2$ cup	**milk**
$^1/_2$ cup	**Italian seasoned bread crumbs**

Roll ham and cheese inside flattened chicken breast. Secure with a toothpick. Place chicken rolls in greased $2^1/_2$ to $3^1/_2$-quart slow cooker. Mix soup with milk and pour over chicken. Sprinkle with bread crumbs. Cover and cook on low heat 6–8 hours. Makes 4–6 servings.

Serve with steamed vegetables and wild rice pilaf.

CHEESY CHICKEN

4 to 6 **boneless, skinless chicken breasts**
2 cans (10.75 ounces each) **cream of chicken soup,** condensed
1 can (10.75 ounces) **cheddar cheese soup,** condensed
1 teaspoon **dried rosemary** or **dill**

Place chicken in greased 4$\frac{1}{2}$ to 6-quart slow cooker. In a bowl, combine remaining ingredients and pour over chicken. Cover and cook on low heat 6–8 hours or on high heat 3–4 hours. Makes 8–10 servings.

Serve over hot cooked noodles or rice with a side of steamed vegetables.

CHICKEN AND DRESSING

4 to 6	**boneless, skinless chicken breasts**
1 can (10.75 ounces)	**cream of chicken soup,** condensed
$1/3$ cup	**milk**
1 package (6 ounces)	**chicken-flavored stuffing mix**
1 $2/3$ cups	**water**

Place chicken in greased $4^1/2$ to 6-quart slow cooker. In a separate bowl, combine soup and milk, then pour over chicken. Combine stuffing mix and water. Spoon over chicken and soup mixture. Cover and cook on low heat 6–8 hours. Makes 4–6 servings.

Serve with buttery steamed carrots sprinkled with dried basil.

CITRUS-GLAZED CHICKEN

4	**boneless, skinless chicken breasts**
$1/3$ cup	**orange juice**
3 tablespoons	**brown sugar**
$1/8$ teaspoon	**salt**
I tablespoon	**cornstarch**

Place chicken in greased 3 to $4^1/_2$-quart slow cooker. Pour orange juice over chicken. Sprinkle brown sugar and salt over top. Cover and cook on low heat 6–9 hours. Remove chicken with slotted spoon or spatula.

Pour liquid from slow cooker into a small saucepan. Stir in cornstarch with a whisk. Over medium heat, bring to a boil, stirring until sauce thickens. Pour glaze over chicken. Makes 4 servings.

Serve with twice-baked potatoes and a green salad.

CREAMY BLACK BEAN SALSA CHICKEN

2 to 4	**boneless, skinless chicken breasts**
1 cup	**chicken broth**
1 cup	**salsa**
1 can (15 ounces)	**corn,** drained
1 can (15 ounces)	**black beans,** drained
1 package	**taco seasoning**
$1/2$ cup	**sour cream**
1 cup	**grated cheddar cheese**

Place chicken in greased $3^1/2$ to 5-quart slow cooker. Pour broth, salsa, corn, beans, and taco seasoning over chicken. Cover and cook on low heat 6–8 hours or on high heat 3–4 hours. Remove chicken with slotted spoon and place on serving dish. Stir sour cream and cheese into sauce in slow cooker, then pour over chicken. Makes 3–5 servings.

Serve with warm flour tortillas and Spanish rice.

TERISHA'S CHICKEN

4 to 6	**boneless, skinless chicken breasts**
1 cup	**soy sauce**
1 cup	**sugar**
1 teaspoon	**garlic salt**
1/2 cup	**chopped onion***

Place chicken in greased 4 1/2 to 6-quart slow cooker. In a saucepan, combine soy sauce, sugar, garlic salt, and onion. Bring to a boil then pour sauce over chicken in slow cooker. Cover and cook on low heat 6–8 hours or on high heat 3–4 hours. Makes 4–6 servings.

Serve with fettuccine Alfredo and steamed California-blend vegetables.

* 1/4 cup dried minced onion can be substituted.

GREEK PITA CHICKEN SANDWICHES

2 to 4	**boneless, skinless chicken breasts**
1	**medium sweet onion,** thinly sliced
$^1/_2$ teaspoon	**minced garlic**
1$^1/_2$ teaspoons	**lemon pepper seasoning**
$^1/_2$ teaspoon	**dried oregano**
$^1/_4$ teaspoon	**allspice**
$^1/_2$ cup	**plain yogurt**
	pita bread, cut in half

Place chicken in greased 2$^1/_2$ to 3$^1/_2$-quart slow cooker. Lay onion over chicken and sprinkle with seasonings. Cover and cook on low heat 6–8 hours. Break chicken apart with two forks and stir in yogurt. Spoon into warm pita bread halves. Garnish with Roma tomato and cucumber slices. Makes 6–8 servings.

Serve with salad greens topped with crumbled feta cheese and olives.

HONEY-MUSTARD CHICKEN STIR-FRY

2	**large boneless, skinless chicken breasts**
1 1/2 cups	**teriyaki marinade**
1/3 cup	**water**
1 bottle (18 ounces)	**honey-mustard barbecue sauce**
1 bag (16 ounces)	**frozen California-blend vegetables**

Marinate chicken overnight in teriyaki marinade.* Place marinated chicken breasts and water in greased 3 to 4 1/2-quart slow cooker. Discard marinade. Cover and cook on low heat 6–8 hours. Break chicken into chunks with a knife. Pour barbecue sauce over chicken chunks. Stir in frozen vegetables. Cover and cook on high heat 30–60 minutes or until vegetables are heated completely through. Makes 4–6 servings.

Serve over cooked brown or white rice.

* To shorten preparation time, buy pre-marinated chicken breasts from the meat department of your local grocery store.

CHICKEN AND GREEN CHILIES

4 to 6 **boneless, skinless chicken breasts**
1 1/2 cups **chopped onion**
1 can (10.75 ounces) **cream of chicken soup,** condensed
2 cans (4 ounces each) **chopped green chilies,** with liquid

Place chicken in greased 4 1/2 to 6-quart slow cooker. Combine remaining ingredients and pour over chicken. Cover and cook on low heat 6–8 hours or on high heat 3–4 hours. Makes 6–8 servings.

Serve over steamed brown rice and garnish with a dollop of sour cream.

ALL-DAY SALSA CHICKEN

3 to 4	**boneless, skinless chicken breasts**
I jar (16 ounces)	**chunky salsa**
I can (10.5 ounces)	**cream of chicken soup,** condensed

Place chicken breasts in greased 3 to 4^1/$_2$-quart slow cooker. In a bowl, combine salsa and soup. Pour mixture over chicken. Cover and cook on low heat 6–8 hours. Makes 4–6 servings.

Serve on a bed of rice pilaf and top with grated pepper jack cheese.

HONEY-MUSTARD CHICKEN WINGS

3 pounds	**chicken wings**
I bottle (18 ounces)	**honey-mustard barbecue sauce***
I teaspoon	**minced garlic**
I teaspoon	**dried rosemary**
2 to 3 tablespoons	**cornstarch**
2 to 3 tablespoons	**brown sugar**

Place chicken wings in greased 3^1/$_2$ to 4^1/$_2$-quart slow cooker. Pour barbecue sauce over chicken. Sprinkle garlic and rosemary over top. Cover and cook on low heat 6–8 hours or on high heat 3–4 hours. Remove chicken wings with slotted spoon.

Drain juice into a 2-quart saucepan. Whisk in cornstarch and brown sugar. Bring to a boil.

Return chicken to slow cooker, and drizzle glaze over meat. Wings can be kept on warm or low setting and served directly from slow cooker. Makes 10–15 servings.

Serve with ranch and bleu cheese dipping sauces.

* Original or honey-flavored barbecue sauce can be substituted.

CHICKEN STROGANOFF

2 to 3	**boneless, skinless chicken breasts**
I can (4 ounces)	**mushroom pieces,** drained*
I can (10.5 ounces)	**cream of mushroom soup,** condensed
I tablespoon	**soy sauce**
I carton (16 ounces)	**sour cream**

Place chicken in greased $2^1/2$ to 4-quart slow cooker. Pour mushrooms, soup, and soy sauce over chicken. Cover and cook on low heat 6–8 hours or on high heat 3–4 hours. Break up chicken with two forks. Stir in sour cream. Cover and cook on low heat 15–30 minutes. Makes 4–6 servings.

Serve over hot cooked wide egg noodles.

* $^1/2$ cup fresh sliced mushrooms can be substituted.

CATALINA APRICOT CHICKEN

4 to 6 **boneless, skinless chicken breasts**
1 cup **Catalina salad dressing**
1 package **dried onion soup mix**
1 cup **apricot jam** or **preserves**

Place chicken in greased 3^1/$_2$ to 5-quart slow cooker. In bowl, combine salad dressing, onion soup mix, and preserves. Pour over chicken. Cover and cook on low heat 6–8 hours. Do not cook on high heat. Makes 4–6 servings.

Serve over hot cooked rice with a fresh garden salad.

LEMON-HONEY CHICKEN

2 **boneless, skinless chicken breasts**
3/4 teaspoon **ginger**
1/4 cup **lemon juice**
1/2 cup **honey**

Place chicken in greased 1 1/2 to 2 1/2-quart slow cooker. Mix ginger, lemon juice, and honey together. Drizzle over chicken. Cover and cook on low heat 6–8 hours or on high heat 3–4 hours. Makes 2–3 servings.

Serve over angel hair pasta and oriental vegetables.

* Sauce can be thickened by adding small amounts of instant potato flakes until it reaches desired consistency.

CHICKEN ALFREDO LASAGNA

12	**lasagna noodles,** uncooked
2 jars (16 ounces each)	**Alfredo sauce**
$1/3$ cup	**water**
$1 1/2$ cups	**chicken,** cooked and diced
1 carton (16 ounces)	**ricotta** or **cottage cheese**
2 cups	**grated mozzarella cheese**

Break 4 noodles to fit in bottom of greased 6 to 7-quart slow cooker. Layer a third of Alfredo sauce, half of water, and half of chicken over noodles. Spread half of ricotta or cottage cheese and sprinkle a third of mozzarella over meat layer. Add another layer of noodles. Layer a third of Alfredo sauce, remaining chicken, water, and ricotta or cottage cheese. Sprinkle second third of mozzarella. Layer remaining noodles, sauce, and mozzarella. Cover and cook on low heat 4–5 hours. Do not cook more than 5 hours. Makes 10–12 servings.

Serve with hot garlic bread.

VARIATION: Add a small can (2.25 ounces) of sliced olives between layers.

WILD RICE AND CHICKEN

2 cans (10.75 ounces each)	**cream of chicken soup,** condensed
2 cups	**water**
2 boxes (4.3 ounces each)	**seasoned long-grain and wild rice,** with seasoning packets
4	**boneless, skinless chicken breasts**

Combine soup, water, rice, and seasoning packets.* Pour half of rice mixture into greased 3^1/$_2$ to 4^1/$_2$-quart slow cooker. Lay chicken on top of rice. Pour remaining rice mixture over chicken. Cover and cook on low heat 6–7 hours or on high heat 3–4 hours. Do not overcook or rice will become mushy. Makes 4–6 servings.

Serve with a spinach salad topped with apple chunks and raspberry vinaigrette.

* Rice will expand during cooking time. Do not cook this recipe in a slow cooker smaller than 3^1/$_2$ quarts.

Beef

BEEFY CORNBREAD CASSEROLE

1 pound	**lean ground beef,** browned and drained
1	**medium onion,** chopped
1 can (10.75 ounces)	**tomato soup,** condensed
1 can (15.25 ounces)	**whole kernel corn,** drained
1 to 2 tablespoons	**chili powder**
1 teaspoon	**salt**
$^1/_2$ cup	**water**

Topping:

1 pouch (6.5 ounces)	**cornbread mix**
1	**egg**
2 tablespoons	**butter** or **margarine,** melted
$^1/_3$ cup	**milk**
$^1/_2$ cup	**grated cheddar cheese**

Place beef and onion in greased 3 to 4$^1/_2$-quart slow cooker. Stir in soup, corn, chili powder, salt, and water.

In a separate bowl, mix cornbread mix, egg, butter, and milk together. Spread batter evenly over the top of meat mixture. Cover and cook on low heat 5–6 hours or until toothpick inserted in the center comes out clean. Sprinkle cheese over top for last 15 minutes of cooking, if desired. Makes 6–8 servings.

This recipe can be easily doubled by using a 6 to 7-quart slow cooker.

FAMILY FAVORITE CASSEROLE

I pound	**ground beef,** browned and drained
I	**medium onion,** chopped
1 1/2 cups	**diced potatoes**
1 1/2 cups	**baby carrots,** cut in thirds
1/2 teaspoon	**salt**
I can (10.5 ounces)	**cream of mushroom soup,** condensed
1/2 cup	**milk**
1 1/2 cups	**elbow macaroni,** cooked
2 cups	**grated cheddar cheese**

Combine all ingredients except milk, macaroni, and cheese in greased
3 1/2 to 5-quart slow cooker. Stir to combine. Cover and cook on low
heat 6–10 hours or on high heat 3–4 hours. Stir in milk and cooked
macaroni during the last 30 minutes of cooking if on low heat or the
last 15 minutes if on high heat. Sprinkle grated cheese over top. Makes
6–8 servings.

Serve with buttery steamed asparagus.

STUFFED PASTA SHELLS

1/2 pound	**ground beef,** browned and drained
1/2 cup	**onion,** chopped
1 cup	**grated mozzarella cheese**
1/4 cup	**seasoned bread crumbs**
1 teaspoon	**minced garlic**
1 1/2 teaspoons	**dried parsley**
1	**egg,** beaten
18	**jumbo pasta shells,** partially cooked*
2 jars (15.5 ounces each)	**spaghetti sauce**
1/2 cup	**grated Parmesan cheese**

Combine beef, onion, mozzarella, bread crumbs, garlic, parsley, and egg. Stuff partially cooked pasta shells with spoonful of meat mixture. Pour one jar of spaghetti sauce in greased 4 1/2 to 6-quart slow cooker. Place stuffed shells on top of sauce. Pour remaining sauce evenly over pasta. Sprinkle with Parmesan cheese. Cover and cook on low heat 4–5 hours. Do not overcook. Makes 4–6 servings.

Serve with Caesar salad and garlic bread.

* Only cook jumbo shells 7 minutes in boiling water. They will become mushy if overcooked.

GRANDMA BRENDA'S FRITO PIE

$^1/_2$ pound	**ground beef,** browned and drained
2 cans (16 ounces)	**pork and beans,** pork removed
1 can (4 ounces)	**chopped green chilies**
1 can (8 ounces)	**tomato sauce**
4 to 6 drops	**Tabasco sauce**
1 bag (15 ounces)	**Fritos corn chips**

Combine all ingredients except chips in greased 3 to 4$^1/_2$-quart slow cooker. Cover and cook on low heat 6–8 hours or on high heat 3–4 hours. Scoop over a handful of Fritos. Makes 6–8 servings.

Serve with shredded lettuce, diced tomato, sour cream, and grated cheddar cheese.

MOUTHWATERING MEAT LOAF

2 pounds	**extra lean ground beef**
$1/3$ cup	**chopped green pepper**
$1/3$ cup	**chopped onion***
I can (8 ounces)	**tomato sauce**
I	**egg,** beaten
I cup	**quick oats**

In a mixing bowl, combine all ingredients. Shape into a loaf and place in greased $3^1/2$ to 5-quart slow cooker. Cover and cook on low heat 6–8 hours or until meat thermometer reads 165 degrees. Turn off slow cooker and wait 10–15 minutes before serving. Makes 6–8 servings.

Serve with baked potatoes topped with sour cream and chives.

* $1/4$ cup dried minced onion can be substituted.

GRANDMA'S SAUCY MEAT LOAF

1 1/2 pounds	**ground beef**
3/4 cup	**quick oats**
1	**egg,** beaten
3/4 cup	**milk**
1/4 teaspoon	**black pepper**
1/4 cup	**dried minced onion**

Topping:
2/3 cup	**ketchup**
1 tablespoon	**brown sugar**
1 tablespoon	**mustard**

In a large bowl, combine beef, oats, egg, milk, pepper, and onion. Shape into a loaf and place in greased 2 1/2 to 3 1/2-quart slow cooker. Mix together ketchup, brown sugar, and mustard. Spread over top. Cover and cook on low heat 6–8 hours or until meat thermometer reads 165 degrees. Makes 4–6 servings.

Serve with garlic mashed potatoes.

BARBECUE MEAT LOAF

3 pounds	**ground beef**
1 1/2 cups	**quick oats**
2	**eggs,** beaten
1 1/4 cups	**milk**
1/2 teaspoon	**black pepper**
1/2 cup	**dried minced onion**
1 bottle (16 ounces)	**barbecue sauce,** divided

In a large bowl, combine beef, oats, eggs, milk, pepper, onion, and half of barbecue sauce. Press meat mixture into a greased 5 to 7-quart slow cooker. Spread remaining barbecue sauce over top. Cover and cook on low heat 6–8 hours or until meat thermometer reads 165 degrees. Makes 10–12 servings.

Serve with french fries or onion rings.

HOT MEATBALL SUBS

1 package (18 ounces)	**frozen cooked meatballs***
1 jar (26 ounces)	**chunky garden–style spaghetti sauce**
1/2 teaspoon	**minced garlic,** optional
	Monterey Jack or **mozzarella cheese,** sliced
	hoagie buns

Combine meatballs, spaghetti sauce, and garlic, if desired, in greased 2 to 3 1/2-quart slow cooker. Cook on low heat 4–6 hours. Place meatballs and desired amount of sauce on bun. Lay cheese slices on top of meat. Makes 6–8 servings.

Serve with tossed green salad and potato chips.

* Can use 25–28 frozen precooked homemade meatballs for this recipe.

CHILI DOGS

¹/₂ to 1 pound	**ground beef,** browned and drained
2 cans (15 ounces each)	**chili with beans**
1 cup	**chopped onion***
1 teaspoon	**oregano**
1 teaspoon	**chili powder**
1 teaspoon	**cumin**
¹/₂ teaspoon	**minced garlic**
1 package (16 ounces)	**hot dogs**
	hot dog buns

Combine beef, chili, onion, and remaining seasonings in greased 3 to
4¹/₂-quart slow cooker. Cover and cook on low heat 6–8 hours or on
high heat 3–4 hours. Makes 8–10 servings.

Cook hot dogs immediately before serving. Place hot dog in bun.
Spoon chili over hot dog. Garnish with grated cheese and fresh
chopped onion.

Serve with seasoned potato wedges.

* ¹/₂ cup dried minced onion can be substituted.

MANDARIN ORANGE STEAKS

2 pounds	**boneless beef steaks**
1 1/2 cups	**orange juice**
1/2 cup	**fresh lemon juice**
1 teaspoon	**hot sauce**
1 can (11 ounces)	**mandarin oranges,** drained and chilled

Place steaks in greased 2 to 3 1/2-quart slow cooker. Combine orange juice, lemon juice, and hot sauce and pour over steaks. Cover and cook on low heat 8–10 hours. Makes 4–6 servings.

Serve topped with chilled mandarin oranges over hot cooked rice.

GINGERALE POT ROAST

1 bag (16 ounces)	**baby carrots**
4 to 6	**russet potatoes,** peeled and cubed
3 to 4 pound	**rump roast**
1/2	**medium onion,** thinly sliced
1 envelope	**brown gravy mix**
1 envelope	**onion soup mix**
2 cups	**gingerale***

Place carrots and potatoes in greased 4 to 6-quart slow cooker. Place roast over top. Lay onion on top of roast. Dissolve gravy and soup mixes into gingerale and pour over meat. Cover and cook on low heat 8–10 hours. Makes 6–8 servings.

Serve with spinach, craisin, and apple salad drizzled with apple cider vinaigrette dressing.

* Do not use diet gingerale.

ITALIAN BEEF ROAST

1 bag (16 ounces) **baby carrots**
4 to 6 **russet potatoes,** peeled and cubed
2 to 3 pound **beef roast**
$1/2$ **onion,** thinly sliced
1 cup **Italian salad dressing**

Place carrots and potatoes in bottom of greased $4^1/2$ to 6-quart slow cooker. Place beef over top. Lay onion on top of roast. Pour dressing over the top of meat. Cover and cook on low heat 8–10 hours. Makes 6–8 servings.

Serve with your favorite focaccia bread and fruit salad.

SHREDDED BEEF AND ROOTBEER SANDWICHES

3 to 4 pound	**extra lean boneless beef roast**
I can (12 ounces)	**rootbeer***
1 1/2 cups	**barbecue sauce**
	hamburger buns

Place roast in greased 3 1/2 to 5-quart slow cooker. Mix rootbeer and barbecue sauce together in a bowl. Pour over roast. Cover and cook on low heat 8–10 hours. Shred roast with two forks. Scoop onto toasted hamburger buns. Makes 10–12 servings.

Serve with a fresh fruit platter.

* Do not use diet rootbeer.

SWEET-AND-SOUR MEATBALLS

2 packages (18 ounces each)	**frozen cooked meatballs**
1 can (14 ounces)	**crushed pineapple,** with juice
1 cup	**brown sugar**
3 tablespoons	**soy sauce**
1 tablespoon	**cornstarch**
1 tablespoon	**water**

Place frozen meatballs in greased 3 1/2 to 4-quart slow cooker. In a saucepan, combine pineapple with juice, brown sugar, and soy sauce. Bring mixture to a boil, stirring frequently.

In a small bowl, mix cornstarch and water together, then add to simmering sauce to thicken. Pour sauce over meatballs. Cover and cook on low heat 3–4 hours. Makes 10–15 servings.

Meatballs can be served on a platter with toothpicks as appetizers, or over hot cooked white rice garnished with chow mein noodles as a main dish.

SWEET-AND-TANGY TWISTED BEEF

2 pounds **stew beef***
$^1/_4$ cup **brown sugar**
$^1/_4$ cup **soy sauce**
1 cup **salsa**

Combine all ingredients in greased $3^1/_2$ to 5-quart slow cooker. Cover and cook on low heat 7–9 hours or on high heat 4 hours. Makes 6–8 servings.

Serve over hot cooked white or brown rice with your favorite egg roll.

VARIATION: Add $^3/_4$ cup frozen kernel corn during the last 30–40 minutes of cooking.

* Pork or chicken stew meat can be substituted.

MEXICAN ROAST

3 pound **roast,** any kind
2 tablespoons **taco seasoning**
1 jar (16 ounces) **salsa**

Place meat in greased 3$\frac{1}{2}$ to 5-quart slow cooker. Sprinkle taco seasoning over meat. Pour salsa over top. Cover and cook on low heat 10–12 hours or on high heat 5–6 hours. Makes 6–8 servings.

Serve with Spanish rice and your favorite steamed vegetables. Leftovers can be shredded to use in tacos, burritos, or enchiladas.

PORK

SWEET PORK RIBS

I pound	**baby back pork ribs**
I cup	**barbecue sauce**
I jar (18 ounces)	**cherry jam** or **preserves**
1 1/2 tablespoons	**Dijon mustard**
1/2 teaspoon	**salt**
1/2 teaspoon	**pepper**

Place ribs in greased 2 to 3 1/2-quart slow cooker. In a bowl, combine remaining ingredients. Pour sauce over ribs. Cover and cook on low heat 6–8 hours or on high heat 3–4 hours. Makes 2–4 servings.

Serve with seasoned potato wedges and steamed zucchini.

ORANGE-GLAZED PORK RIBS

2 pounds	**country-style boneless pork ribs**
1	**large onion,** thinly sliced
1 cup	**orange marmalade**
1/3 cup	**chopped green pepper**
1/4 cup	**soy sauce**
1 teaspoon	**minced garlic**
1/2 teaspoon	**ground ginger**

Place ribs in greased 3 1/2 to 5-quart slow cooker. Lay onion slices over ribs. Combine remaining ingredients in a bowl. Spread sauce over ribs. Cover and cook on low heat 6–8 hours or on high heat 3–4 hours. Makes 4–6 servings.

Serve with wild rice and mushroom pilaf.

ALOHA PORK CHOPS

4 to 5	**boneless pork chops**
$1/2$	**green bell pepper,** seeded and diced
1	**medium onion,** chopped*
I can (20 ounces)	**crushed pineapple,** drained
I bottle (18 ounces)	**honey-mustard barbecue sauce**

Place pork chops in greased $4^{1}/_{2}$ to 6-quart slow cooker. Sprinkle bell pepper and onion over meat. Spread drained pineapple over top. Pour barbecue sauce evenly over pineapple. Cover and cook on low heat 6–8 hours or on high heat 3–4 hours. Cut meat into chunks. Makes 4–6 servings.

Serve over hot cooked brown rice with a green salad topped with mandarin oranges and toasted slivered almonds.

* $1/2$ cup dried minced onion can be substituted.

CRANBERRY-SAUCED COCKTAIL SAUSAGES

2 packages (16 ounces each)	**little smoked sausages**
1 cup	**chili sauce**
1 cup	**barbecue sauce**
3/4 cup	**jellied cranberry sauce**

Place sausages in greased 2 1/2 to 3 1/2-quart slow cooker. Combine remaining ingredients and pour over meat. Cover and cook on low heat 1 1/2–3 hours. Makes 16 servings.

Serve as an appetizer.

HONEY-MUSTARD PORK

4 to 5	**pork chops**
$^1/_2$ cup	**flour**
$^1/_4$ teaspoon	**black pepper**
1 teaspoon	**mustard**
1 can (10.75 ounces)	**chicken with rice soup,** condensed
1 soup can	**water**

Dip pork chops in flour and place in greased 4$^1/_2$ to 6-quart slow cooker. Sprinkle pepper over meat. In a separate bowl, mix mustard, soup, and water together. Pour soup mixture over meat. Cover and cook on low heat 6–8 hours or on high heat 3–4 hours. Remove pork chops with slotted spoon and place on a serving tray.

In a blender, puree the liquid left in slow cooker 30–60 seconds to make gravy. Makes 4–5 servings.

Serve with mashed potatoes.

PORK CHOP STROGANOFF

4	**boneless pork chops**
I can (4 ounces)	**mushrooms,** drained
I can (10.5 ounces)	**cream of mushroom soup,** condensed
I cup	**sour cream**
I bag (8 ounces)	**pasta**

Place pork chops in greased 3 1/2 to 5-quart slow cooker. Layer mushrooms over meat. Spread soup over top, then cover and cook on low heat 6–8 hours. Using a knife and fork, cut pork chops into bite-sized pieces. Stir sour cream into meat sauce. Cover and leave on low heat while preparing pasta according to package directions. Stir hot cooked noodles into the sauce and serve. Makes 4–6 servings.

Serve with a green bean and onion medley.

POLYNESIAN HAM STEAKS

2 slices	**boneless ham,** fully cooked (about $3/4$-inch thick each)
2 tablespoons	**brown sugar**
1 tablespoon	**Dijon mustard**
6	**pineapple slices**

Place ham in greased $2^1/2$ to $3^1/2$-quart slow cooker. Combine brown sugar and mustard in separate bowl, then spread over ham. Place pineapple slices over top. Cover and cook on low heat 6 hours or on high heat 3 hours. Makes 4–6 servings.

Serve with a fruit salad and potato roll.

Can easily be doubled using a 4 to 6-quart slow cooker.

CHEESY POTATO-AND-HAM CASSEROLE

Bottom Layer:

I package (32 ounces)	**frozen hash brown potatoes,** cubed or shredded
I tablespoon	**dried chopped onion**
I teaspoon	**salt**
I carton (8 ounces)	**sour cream**
I can (10.75 ounces)	**cream of chicken soup,** condensed
2 cups	**grated cheddar cheese**
2 cups	**chopped cooked ham**

Topping:

$^1/_4$ cup	**butter** or **margarine,** melted
I package (6 ounces)	**herb-seasoning stuffing mix**

Combine bottom layer ingredients in a greased $4^1/_2$ to 6-quart slow cooker. Sprinkle stuffing mix over top, then drizzle on butter. Cover and cook on low heat 5–6 hours or on high heat $2^1/_2$–4 hours. Makes 10–12 servings.

Serve with French-cut green beans.

SPICY RICE CASSEROLE

4 cups	**boiling water**
4	**beef bouillon cubes**
24 ounces	**pork sausage**
I teaspoon	**garlic powder**
2 teaspoons	**ground cumin**
4	**medium onions,** chopped
4	**medium green peppers,** chopped
I can (4 ounces)	**chopped jalapeños,** drained
2 packages (6.25 ounces each)	**long-grain converted and wild rice mix,** with seasoning packets

Pour hot water into greased 6 to 7-quart slow cooker already set on high heat. Stir in bouillon cubes. Brown sausage, garlic powder, and cumin in skillet. Drain. Add onions and green peppers, saute until vegetables are tender (5–7 minutes). Transfer to slow cooker. Stir in jalapeño peppers, rice, and seasoning packets. Cover and cook on low heat 4–5 hours. Do not overcook. Makes 8–10 servings.

Serve with warm cheese bread.

SUPREME PIZZA LASAGNA

12	**lasagna noodles**
1 teaspoon	**Italian seasoning**
12 ounces	**sausage,** browned and drained
24	**pepperoni slices**
2 jars (26–28 ounces each)	**chunky spaghetti sauce,** with mushrooms*
1/4 cup	**water**
1 carton (16 ounces)	**ricotta** or **cottage cheese**
2 cups	**grated mozzarella cheese**

Break 4 noodles to fit in bottom of greased 6 to 7-quart slow cooker. Stir Italian seasoning into browned sausage and spread half of mixture over the noodles in slow cooker. Lay 12 pepperoni slices over sausage. Then layer a third of the spaghetti sauce, half of the water, half of the ricotta cheese, and a third of the mozzarella cheese over meat. Add another layer of noodles, browned sausage, pepperoni, and a third of the spaghetti sauce. Spread remaining water and ricotta cheese over sauce, then another third of the mozzarella. Layer remaining noodles, sauce, and mozzarella over top. Cover and cook on low heat 4–5 hours. Do not overcook. Makes 10–12 servings.

Serve with a tossed garden salad and breadsticks.

* Spaghetti sauce with green peppers and onions can also be used.

SOUTHWESTERN PORK WRAPS

2 to 3 pound	**boneless pork loin roast**
3 cans (4 ounces each)	**chopped green chilies,** with liquid
I can (8 ounces)	**tomato sauce**
$2/3$ cup	**barbecue sauce**
I	**large sweet onion,** thinly sliced
$1/4$ cup	**chili powder**
I teaspoon	**ground cumin**
I teaspoon	**dried oregano**
	flavored tortillas

Place roast in greased $3^1/2$ to 4-quart slow cooker. In a separate bowl,
combine all other ingredients except tortillas and spread over roast.
Cover and cook on low heat 8–10 hours or on high heat 4–5 hours.
When done, shred roast with two forks. Makes 8–10 servings.

Wrap meat in a flavored tortilla with a thin slice of tomato, green leaf
lettuce, and a dollop of sour cream.

ASIAN PORK WRAPS

2 1/2 to 3 pound	**boneless pork loin roast**
2/3 cup	**hoisin sauce***
2 teaspoons	**minced garlic**
1 teaspoon	**ground ginger**
1/2 teaspoon	**Chinese five-spice powder**

Place roast in greased 3 1/2 to 5-quart slow cooker. Mix remaining ingredients in a bowl and spread over top. Cover and cook on low heat 6–8 hours. Shred roast with two forks. Makes 8–10 servings.

Serve on warm whole wheat tortillas with sliced green onion, mandarin oranges, toasted slivered almonds, and shredded lettuce.

* Hoisin sauce can be found in the Asian/Oriental section of your supermarket.

SAUSAGE CASSEROLE

12 ounces	**sausage,** browned and drained
I envelope (1.5 ounces)	**chicken soup mix**
$^3/_4$ cup	**long-grain white rice,** not instant
2	**celery stalks,** diced
$^1/_3$ cup	**slivered almonds**
4 cups	**water**
	salt and pepper, to taste

Combine all ingredients in greased $4^1/_2$ to 6-quart slow cooker and stir well. Cover and cook on low heat 4–5 hours or until rice is tender. Makes 6–8 servings.

Serve with a broccoli and cauliflower medley.

APPLE-CRANBERRY PORK CHOPS

4 **boneless pork chops**
I can (16 ounces) **whole cranberry sauce**
$^3/_4$ cup **applesauce**

Place pork chops in greased 2 to $3^1/_2$-quart slow cooker. Spread cranberry sauce over top. Pour in applesauce. Cover and cook on low heat 6–8 hours or on high heat 3–4 hours. Makes 4 servings.

Serve over hot cooked white rice with a green salad and a dinner roll.

PORK ROAST WITH APRICOT DIJON MUSTARD

2¹/₂ to 3 pound	**boneless pork roast**
1	**medium onion,** thinly sliced
1 jar (16 ounces)	**apricot jam** or **preserves**
3 tablespoons	**Dijon mustard**

Place roast in greased 2 to 3¹/₂-quart slow cooker. Lay onion slices over roast. In a bowl, combine jam and mustard and spread over top. Cover and cook on low heat 6–8 hours or on high heat 3–4 hours or until internal meat temperature reaches 165 degrees. Makes 5–6 servings.

Serve with French bread.

DESSERTS

COUNTRY PEACHES

I can (29 ounces)	**sliced peaches,** drained with juice reserved
$^2/_3$ cup	**old-fashioned oatmeal** (not instant)
I cup	**Bisquick**
$^1/_2$ teaspoon	**cinnamon**
$^1/_2$ cup	**brown sugar,** firmly packed

Pour peaches into greased $2^1/_2$ to $3^1/_2$-quart slow cooker. Mix oatmeal, Bisquick, and peach juice together in a large bowl and spoon over peaches. Sprinkle cinnamon and brown sugar over top. Cover and cook on low heat 3 hours. Makes 6–8 servings.

Serve warm with a scoop of vanilla ice cream.

GOLDEN APPLE-NUT COBBLER

2 cans (21 ounces each)	**apple pie filling**
1	**white** or **yellow cake mix**
$1/2$ cup	**butter** or **margarine,** melted
$1/3$ cup	**almonds** or **pecans,** chopped

Spread pie filling on bottom of greased $4^1/2$ to 6-quart slow cooker. Sprinkle cake mix over top. Drizzle butter evenly over cake mix, then sprinkle with chopped nuts. Cover and cook on low heat 4 hours or on high heat 2 hours. Makes 10–12 servings.

Serve warm with whipped topping or vanilla ice cream.

VARIATION: Use $1/4$ cup melted butter and $1/3$ cup water in place of $1/2$ cup butter, for a low-fat version.

NUTTY BROWNIES

¹/₄ cup	**butter** or **margarine,** melted
³/₄ cup	**chopped walnuts** or **pecans**
1 family size box (21 ounces)	**brownie mix**
	ingredients on back of box

Pour butter into greased 3¹/₂-quart slow cooker. Sprinkle with half the nuts. Mix brownies according to package directions and pour over nuts, sprinkle rest of nuts over top. Cover and cook on low heat 3–3¹/₂ hours or until done. Let stand 5 minutes. Invert onto serving platter. Makes 10–12 servings.

Serve warm, dusted with powdered sugar and drizzled with chocolate or caramel sauce.

CHERRY-BLACKBERRY COBBLER

I can (21 ounces)	**cherry pie filling**
I can (21 ounces)	**blackberry pie filling**
I	**yellow** or **white cake mix**
2	**eggs**
$^1/_3$ cup	**evaporated milk**
I teaspoon	**cinnamon**

Spread pie filling on bottom of greased $4^1/_2$ to 6-quart slow cooker. In a bowl, mix cake mix, eggs, milk, and cinnamon together. Spoon cake mixture evenly over pie filling. Cover and cook on low heat 3 hours or on high heat I $^1/_2$ hours. Turn off slow cooker and allow cobbler to cool 20 minutes. Makes I0–I2 servings.

Serve warm with a scoop of vanilla ice cream.

VARIATION: Add 2 cans of one flavor pie filling in place of one of each pie filling.

PERFECT PEACH COBBLER

I can (29 ounces) **peach slices,** with juice
I can (21 ounces) **peach pie filling***
I **white** or **yellow cake mix**
$1/2$ teaspoon **cinnamon**
$1/2$ cup **coconut**
$1/8$ cup **butter** or **margarine,** thinly sliced

Pour juice from peaches into a separate bowl. Spread pie filling and peaches on bottom of greased $4^1/2$ to 6-quart slow cooker. Sprinkle cake mix, cinnamon, and coconut over top. Pour peach juice over dry ingredients. Place butter slices over the dry areas. Cover and cook on low heat 4 hours or on high heat 2 hours. Makes 10–12 servings.

Serve warm with vanilla ice cream or whipped topping.

* Apple pie filling can be substituted.

WALNUT-BLACKBERRY DELIGHT

2 cans (21 ounces each) **blackberry pie filling***
1 **yellow cake mix**
$^1/_2$ cup **butter or margarine,** melted
$^2/_3$ cup **chopped walnuts** or **pecans,** optional

Spread pie filling on bottom of greased 3 to 4$^1/_2$-quart slow cooker.
Combine cake mix and butter. Mixture will be crumbly. Pour over pie
filling. Sprinkle top with nuts, if desired. Cover and cook on low heat
4 hours or on high heat 2 hours. Makes 7–9 servings.

Serve warm with vanilla ice cream lightly sprinkled with cinnamon.

* Any flavor pie filling can be substituted.

EASY BLUEBERRY CRISP

2 cans (21 ounces each)	**blueberry pie filling**
2¹/₂ cups	**granola cereal**
1¹/₂ teaspoons	**cinnamon**
¹/₃ cup	**sugar**
¹/₃ cup	**butter** or **margarine,** melted

Place pie filling on bottom of greased 3 to 4¹/₂-quart slow cooker. Sprinkle remaining ingredients over the pie filling in the order listed above. Cover and cook on low heat 3 hours. Makes 7–9 servings.

Serve warm with vanilla ice cream or whipped topping.

PEACHY CHERRY GRANOLA CRISP

1 can (21 ounces) **cherry pie filling**
1 can (15 ounces) **peach slices,** drained
2$^1/_2$ cups **granola cereal**
1 teaspoon **cinnamon**
$^1/_3$ cup **sugar**
$^1/_3$ cup **butter** or **margarine,** melted

Place pie filling and peach slices on bottom of greased 3 to 4$^1/_2$-quart slow cooker. Sprinkle remaining ingredients over top in the order listed above. Cover and cook on low heat 3 hours. Makes 7–9 servings.

Serve warm with vanilla ice cream or whipped topping.

GOOEY CHERRY CHOCOLATE CAKE

2 cans (21 ounces each) **lite cherry pie filling**
1 **milk chocolate cake mix**
$^1/_2$ cup **butter** or **margarine,** melted

Spread pie filling over bottom of greased $4^1/_2$ to 6-quart slow cooker. Sprinkle cake mix over top. Drizzle butter over cake mix, covering as well as possible. Cover and cook on low heat 4 hours or on high heat 2 hours. Turn the slow cooker off and let covered cake sit for half an hour before serving. Makes 10–12 servings.

Garnish with whipped topping and shaved chocolate.

HOT FUDGE BROWNIE CAKE

Bottom layer:

2 cups	**brownie mix**
1	**egg**
1 tablespoon	**vegetable oil**
$^1/_4$ cup	**water**
$^1/_3$ cup	**milk chocolate chips**

Topping:

$^1/_2$ cup	**brown sugar**
2 tablespoons	**baking cocoa**
$^3/_4$ cup	**boiling water**

Combine all bottom layer ingredients in a bowl. Spread batter in greased $2^1/_2$ to $3^1/_2$-quart slow cooker. Mix together topping ingredients, completely dissolving sugar and cocoa in boiling water. Pour over batter. Cover and cook on high heat 2 hours. Turn off slow cooker and allow to sit in slow cooker 30 minutes. Makes 8–10 servings.

Spoon into bowls and serve with a scoop of french vanilla ice cream, hot fudge, and chopped nuts.

DULCE DE LECHE
(SOUTH AMERICAN CARAMEL)

1 can (14 ounces) **sweetened condensed milk**
water

Remove label from milk can. Place can on its side directly into 2^1/$_2$ to 3^1/$_2$-quart slow cooker. Fill slow cooker with water until it is 3 to 4 inches above can. Cover and cook on low heat 8–10 hours. Turn off slow cooker and allow can to cool 40 minutes inside slow cooker. Chill caramel in unopened can in refrigerator until ready to serve. Makes 6 servings.

Caramel can be used as a dip for apple slices and banana chunks, or as a topping for pancakes, crepes, or ice cream.

Warm caramel can also be spread in bottom of premade graham cracker crust and topped with whipped topping.

NOTES

NOTES

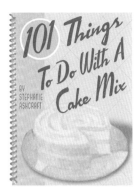

ABOUT THE AUTHORS

Stephanie Ashcraft was raised near Kirklin, Indiana. She received a bachelor's degree in family science and a teaching certificate from Brigham Young University. Stephanie loves teaching, interacting with people, and spending time with friends and family. Since 1998, she has taught cooking classes throughout the state of Utah. She and her husband, Ivan, reside in Rexburg, Idaho with their children. Being a mom is her full-time job.

Janet Eyring was raised in Utah. She received a bachelor's degree in recreation management and youth leadership from Brigham Young University. Janet loves spending time with friends and family and enjoys time away from her kitchen. She teaches a monthly cooking class, Slow-Cooker Sensations, for Macey's Little Cooking Theater in Pleasant Grove, Orem, and Provo, Utah. She and her husband, Sean, reside in Pleasant Grove, Utah, with their children.